A Child's First Library of Learning

Wheels and Wings

TIME-LIFE BOOKS • ALEXANDRIA, VIRGINIA

Contents

How Do You Keep From Falling When You Ride Your Bicycle?

ANSWER The secret is that you must be carefully balanced and keep your bicycle moving forward in order to ride it. If you stop moving, the bicycle cannot be balanced.

■ **Here's the safe way to ride**

If you turn the same way that you're leaning, you won't fall.

If you ride carefully balanced, you won't fall.

■ **Here's the wrong way to ride**

If you turn the other way from the way you're leaning, you'll lose your balance and fall over.

Oops! Look what happens when I stop.

A Few Types of Cycles

▲ Unicycles come in many sizes — from very small to very, very tall.

▶ Here front and rear wheel sizes are different.

▼ A four-wheeler that won't fall if you stop.

▲ Two people can ride and carry their friends along in the sidecar.

TRY THIS

Coin-Rolling Test

Try rolling a coin on its edge. At first it rolls fast and doesn't fall over. But once it slows down it begins to wobble, and then it falls over.

![?] Which Side of the Road Do Cars Go On?

(ANSWER) The answer depends on where you live. In most
countries we drive on the right side of the
road. But in some countries we drive on the left.

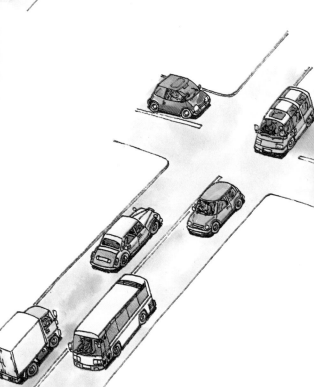

In the United States and Europe we drive on the right.

In Great Britain and Japan we drive on the left.

Steering Wheels Are Different Too.

In the United States and Europe the steering wheel is on the left.

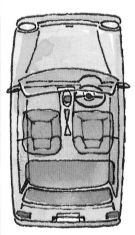

In Japan and Great Britain the steering wheel is on the right.

It is safest when the driver can easily see the oncoming traffic.

● **To the Parent**

The custom of driving on the right was first developed in the United States. Certain kinds of carts and wagons had a place on the left for the driver to sit. To see other drivers it was necessary to drive on the right. When automobiles were first built in the United States the steering wheels were put on the left, and the rule of traffic keeping to the right continued. Since so many cars were built in the U. S., many countries followed this practice. Some countries, however, opted for the British tradition in which the traffic stays to the left. In this book you will find examples of each.

? Why Do We Need Traffic Lights?

ANSWER Roads can become very crowded. When two roads cross, traffic signals are one way of deciding who is to go first. If we did not have these signals there would be many more automobile accidents.

■ Here Are Some Traffic Lights

Traffic lights look very different from one place to another. No matter how they look, however, rules are the same. Red always means "stop," and green always means "go."

▲ United States   ▲ China   ▲ Liechtenstein

The picture above shows what can happen to cars if there is no traffic signal. Below you can see how hard it is for people to cross the street.

▲ Norway

▲ Great Britain

❓ Why Do Fire Engines Use Sirens When They Go to a Fire?

ANSWER Fire engines have to rush to where the fire is. They use their sirens to warn people to get out of the way so they can go faster and not have to stop.

■ Fire engines are always in a hurry

When they are racing to fires they will go through red lights if the way is clear.

If there is a traffic jam they sometimes drive on the other side of the street.

Here Are Some Other Vehicles That Use Sirens to Clear Traffic

Ambulance. It carries people who have been injured, or who are very sick.

Gas company vehicle. It ▶ speeds to dangerous gas leaks or gas fires.

Motorcycle. It rushes police to accidents and helps them chase speeders.

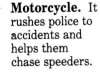

● **To the Parent**

Fire engines must get to the scene of a fire without a moment's delay. That is why, if the way is clear, they continue through any red traffic lights. These emergency vehicles may also drive on the wrong side of the road if necessary. This is also true of police cars and motorcycles, ambulances and other designated vehicles that are equipped with sirens. When any of these vehicles pass in an emergency, ordinary vehicles must slow down or stop, so as to allow them to proceed without impediment. Pedestrians must also give way to the preemptive sirens. Even if the green light is in their favor, they are required to wait for emergency vehicles to pass before they cross the street.

❓ **What Makes Cars Move?**

ANSWER Gasoline explodes inside the engine of a car. This creates a great amount of power, which is used to make the car's wheels turn.

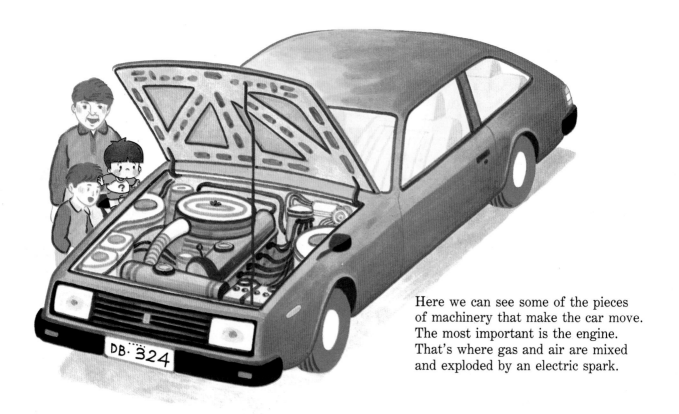

Here we can see some of the pieces of machinery that make the car move. The most important is the engine. That's where gas and air are mixed and exploded by an electric spark.

If a car runs out of gas it will stop.

▲ **Filling station.** Here
is where you fill up
your tank with gas.

◀ **Driver's seat
of a car**

• **To the Parent**

Automotive engines include ordinary gasoline
engines, which are used in passenger cars, the
diesel engines used in trucks and buses, and
engines powered by propane or natural gas.
Engines can also be divided into piston and
rotary types. In a piston engine, a mixture
of gas and air is exploded in the cylinders.
This drives the car's pistons up and down, and
this motion is converted into rotary motion
by the crankshaft and then transmitted by the
driveshaft to the wheels. The rotary engine,
however, can produce rotary motion directly.

❓ Why Are Buses and Some Trucks Flat at the Front?

(ANSWER) The driver's seat in trucks and buses is up high. This makes it easy to see things that are far away but not up close. The flat front makes it easier to see up close.

Trucks that stick out in front are very dangerous. The driver cannot see what is in front of his wheels.

■ Location of the engine

▲ In large trucks the engine is under the driver's seat.

▲ The engine in some cars is found in the rear.

▲ Bus engines are usually in the rear, too.

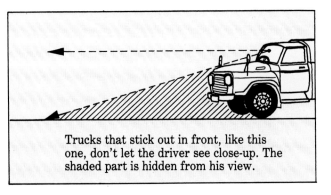

Trucks that stick out in front, like this one, don't let the driver see close-up. The shaded part is hidden from his view.

● **To the Parent**

The hoods covering the engine block on most vintage trucks stuck out in front. Despite the height of the driver's seat, though, this design prevented the driver from seeing the area directly in front of the truck. Finally, to correct this dangerous condition, trucks were redesigned and given flat fronts. This meant that the engine also had to be relocated. The engine is now mounted beneath the driver's seat in most trucks. In buses it normally is at the rear.

Why Do We Put Chains on Cars When It Snows?

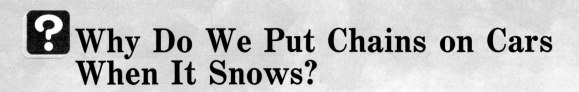

(ANSWER) When a car with ordinary tires tries to go on a snow-covered road it slips and slides. But it doesn't if we put chains on the tires or use special tires with metal spikes.

■ Different kinds of tires

▲ **Bias.** The most common tire.

▲ **Radial.** For safety.

▲ **Rally.** Used for racing.

▲ **Spike.** For snowy roads.

▲ **Tires with chains.** For driving on snowy roads.

Vehicles That Run in Snow

▲ **Snow cat.** It has caterpillar treads instead of wheels so it can run in snow on steep hills. It can even run on soft, new-fallen snow.

▲ **Snowmobile.** It has skis in front for gliding and caterpillar treads in the rear for pushing.

▶ Putting on special snow-racing tires.

▲ **A snow-racing car with special tires**

● To the Parent

When a roadway is covered with snow or ice the wheels of vehicles usually do not come into direct contact with the road's surface. Under conditions like these, ordinary tires will slip on curves or when the brakes are applied. Tire chains are a fairly common way of reducing this danger, but snow tires are also used. On icy roads where snow tires are ineffective, spike tires are used. They have steel studs on them to prevent side-slip and improve safety, but a disadvantage is that they damage the road surface badly. Spike tires are normally mounted on the drive wheels, but in areas of heavy snowfall they may be put on all wheels, and extra chains can be put on the drive wheels to gain an even greater margin of safety.

Why Do Big Trucks Have So Many Tires?

ANSWER Trucks have many tires for carrying heavy loads. Many tires are needed to support extra weight, and so bigger trucks must have more tires. It's the same as when you carry a full shopping bag. It becomes lighter when someone takes one side and you carry it together.

When a load is light not so many tires are needed.

But when a load is heavy more tires are needed.

● **To the Parent**

A truck that has to carry a heavy load needs a very large number of tires to distribute the load's weight evenly. This not only saves wear and tear on the truck itself, but protects the surface of the road as well. Today, giant trailers, like those shown on the opposite page, are being manufactured, and they require an astonishingly large number of tires, as you will see if you try to count them.

Some vehicles have dozens and dozens of tires

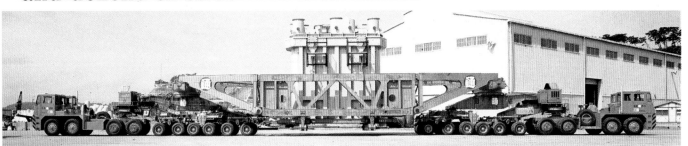

▲ **A 550-ton (500 t) trailer**
It has 184 tires and needs four drivers.
Two drivers move the trailer one way and two the other way.

▲ **A 3,000-ton (2,700 t), self-driven module transport**
It has 864 tires. It moves quite slowly but can carry very, very heavy loads.

Why Does the Drum Of a Ready-Mix Concrete Truck Turn?

ANSWER Ready-mix concrete trucks bring concrete right to the building site. The drum turns so that the concrete will stay well mixed and not begin to harden. If the concrete hardens it cannot be poured out of the mixer.

■ **If the drum turns there's nothing to worry about**

I feel sleepy. I think I'll stop turning and rest a little.

Oh dear! The concrete has become as hard as a rock.

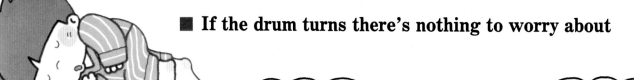

Oh oh! If you don't keep turning the drum, you're going to be sorry.

You didn't keep the drum turning, and just look at what has happened.

■ How the drum looks inside

When the drum is first filled with concrete, it turns in the same direction as the circular arrow.

Loading

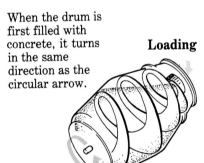

To unload concrete, the drum turns in the other direction, as shown by the circular arrow.

Unloading

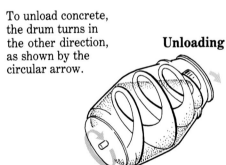

▲ Concrete has many uses, from making swimming pools to building houses. Here workers in a California town use it to make a sidewalk and curb.

● To the Parent

Concrete is made from a mixture of cement, sand, gravel and water. A large building that is under construction requires large amounts of concrete at one time, usually more than is possible to mix at the construction site. That is why concrete is made all together in concrete mixing plants. The ready-mix truck's drum is kept turning as it moves from plant to site so that the concrete stays well mixed and its elements do not separate or solidify.

21

How Is It Possible to Telephone From Inside a Car?

ANSWER Telephones used in cars are called radio telephones. Radio signals sent from the car are picked up by a relay station, which sends them to home telephones.

▲ This transmitter sends out radio signals.

▲ Making a telephone call from a car.

● **To the Parent**

As the car assumes greater importance in our daily life, it is only natural that car telephones should become popular. These telephones operate on radio waves, but are quite different from amateur radio equipment mounted in some cars. While the latter is connected only to other amateur radios, the car telephones are part of the entire telephone system. Car telephones allow people to place and receive calls in their cars and are limited only by the existence of relay stations that connect them with the ordinary telephone circuits. Currently, relay stations are found in urban areas around the world, but the day is quickly approaching when they will cover the countryside as well. Car telephones are especially popular with business commuters, who can conduct business on the way to and from work.

Some other far-out phones

▲ Imagine being so busy that you must talk on two phones at once (above)!

▶ Pay phones in airports are handy for people who travel a lot (above left).

◀ These financial dealers talk with their hands and by phone at the same time.

▲ This phone in the Arizona desert is put there as an aid to motorists who are in trouble and need to telephone for help.

Why Do People Ride in Taxis?

ANSWER Some people do not own cars. They get around in other ways, such as riding on a bus or walking. When people are in a hurry, they often take rides in taxicabs.
A taxi is usually safe, and it can be very convenient. Taxis take you right to where you want to go. Most taxi drivers know the streets very well and can take shortcuts. If you tell the driver that you are in a hurry he usually will try to get you to where you are going as fast and safely as the traffic allows.

Figuring the fare

Taxis charge for their service in different ways. Most have meters. They charge a certain amount for a set distance and extra if you go farther than that. Some cities are broken into zones, and fares are charged by zone. In a few places they bargain with the driver. In many countries a driver also receives a tip for taking you where you wish to go.

A Few Taxis

▲ **A taxi in San Francisco**
The big sign on the roof is used for advertising.

▶ **A taxi in London, England**

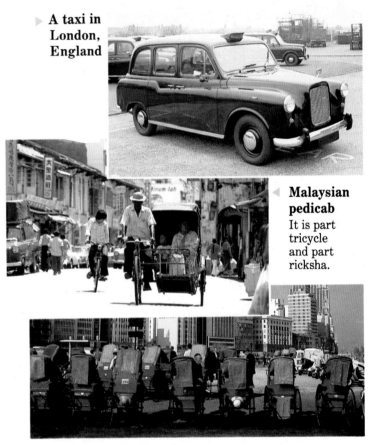

◀ **Malaysian pedicab**
It is part tricycle and part ricksha.

▲ **Rickshas in Hong Kong**

● **To the Parent**

As cities become more and more congested, many people are increasingly reluctant to take their cars into the city. And yet they need a quick way to get around, and the taxi is the answer to their need. Almost all cities of moderate size will have taxicabs. These eliminate the necessity of waiting for buses or walking long distances. They also provide services for people who do not have automobiles of their own. There are many kinds of public conveyances in various countries. Some of them are shown on this page.

? Are Motorcycle Police Everywhere?

ANSWER Many countries have motorcycle police. The motorcycles may differ in color and design, but their job is the same — to catch people who break traffic rules.

Italian police motorcycles are painted black and white.

▲ Police motorcycles in the Netherlands. The one with red is the leader's.

▶ French police motorcycles are black. The signs on the front say "Police."

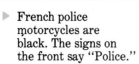

What Colors Are Police Cars in Countries Around the World?

▲ **United Kingdom.** Police cars in Britain are white with an orange and yellow stripe.

▲ **Canada.** The world-famous Mounties now ride in these blue and white patrol cars.

▲ **United States.** Different localities uses different colors for their police cars.

▲ **France.** French police cars are black and white.

▲ **Australia.** The police cars here are solid white.

▲ **Italy.** Italian police cars are grey and white.

● **To the Parent**

With the increase in traffic congestion, motorcycles have come to play an indispensable part in police patrol work. They are used mainly for apprehension of violators of traffic regulations, and their great mobility makes them ideal for the task. Police motorcycles are built to high-performance standards by the world's leading makers: Honda, Suzuki and Yamaha in Japan; Harley-Davidson in the United States; Moto Gucci of Italy and BMW of Germany. Motorcycle duty is more hazardous than patrol car work, and police assigned to it must undergo rigorous training.

Where Can We Travel on Trains?

ANSWER 1 Some trains help us travel around a crowded city. Trains of this type carry many people. Some of these city trains even travel under the ground.

ANSWER 2 Other trains go from one city to other cities. These trains carry fewer people, but they go very fast.

Different Kinds of Seats

Just as there are many kinds of trains, there are many kinds of train seats. Some let you see scenery better, some make it easier to talk, and some can be made into a bed at night. Which one do you like?

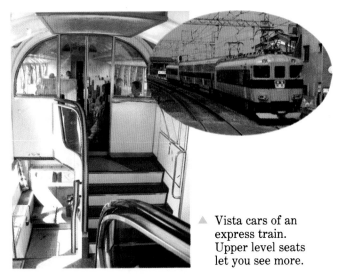

▲ Vista cars of an express train. Upper level seats let you see more.

Panorama cars let you see all around you in every direction.

▲ The seats of this train are plain but comfortable.

▲ Long distance trains may have sleeping cars. At night the seats can be made into beds.

▶ This train has private rooms in which up to four people can sit comfortably.

● **To the Parent**

In spite of the immense popularity of cars and planes, passenger service remains an important aspect of train travel. In crowded urban centers a single commuter train can do the work of 1,000 autos without the accompanying traffic problems. Thousands of commuters in major cities such as New York, London, Paris and Tokyo depend upon an intricate network of trains to get to work every day and back to their homes every evening. Many countries rely on high-speed trains to carry people between cities. In the United States, China and Europe, where trains must often travel considerable distances, train coaches are usually designed to provide passengers maximum comfort. In Japan and many other smaller countries, where routes are shorter, seating in coaches tends to be more crowded.

Why Do Some Trains Have Round Noses?

ANSWER Trains with round noses are called "bullet" trains. Air flows past the nose smoothly. That helps the train go faster. A coupler inside the nose is used to hook trains together. If a train is damaged it is normally hooked to another train and towed away for repair.

▲ With the nose removed the coupler shows just above the blue cowcatcher.

▲ Two "bullet" train engines are shown coupled together nose to nose.

▶ "Bullet" train tracks and wheels are farther apart than those of ordinary trains, so cars are hauled on the flatcars of ordinary trains from the factory to "bullet" train lines. The wider tracks allow the "bullet" trains to go much faster and more smoothly than ordinary trains do.

● To the Parent

Couplers work like the fingertips of two hands clasped together. All trains have couplers, but those on ordinary trains are not covered because wind resistance is not as vital to them as it is to the "bullet" trains, which often hit speeds of 130 miles (210 km) per hour. At that speed, wind creates a drag, which slows trains and levies more power. The round nose eases the drag and streamlines the front of the train. It also accounts for the word "bullet" in the name of this express, which makes it famous the world over.

 What Is the World's Fastest Train?

(ANSWER) The TGV, which in French is "Train Grand Vitesse" or "High-Speed Trains," runs at an average speed of 160 miles (260 km) per hour. The TGV runs in France and holds the world speed record for trains.

Note: SNCF on the front of the TGV is for Société Nationale des Chemins de Fer Français, or French National Railways.

Doesn't it make you feel like riding it?

▲ **Driver's seat.** The wheel is used to control the train's speed.

▲ **First-class passenger coach**

▲ **TGV's buffet car.** Passengers can come here to eat a simple meal.

How Fast They Go

High-speed trains are one of the faster ways to get to where you are going.

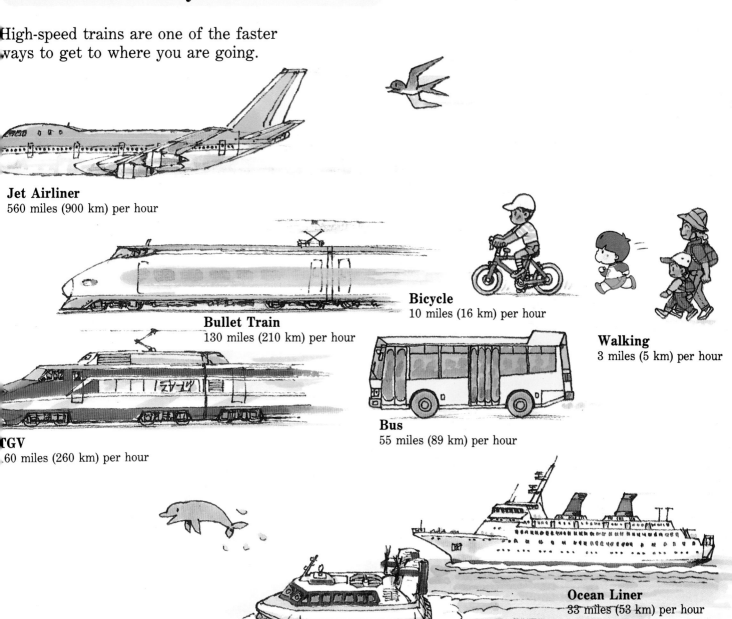

Jet Airliner
560 miles (900 km) per hour

Bullet Train
130 miles (210 km) per hour

TGV
160 miles (260 km) per hour

Bicycle
10 miles (16 km) per hour

Walking
3 miles (5 km) per hour

Bus
55 miles (89 km) per hour

Hovercraft
69 miles (111 km) per hour

Ocean Liner
33 miles (53 km) per hour

■ Pantographs give the trains power

▲ TGV pantographs are bent in two.

▲ Pantographs on "bullet" trains have two arms.

❓ How Are Trains Steered?

ANSWER Cars have a steering wheel so that the driver can turn them. But trains don't need steering wheels because they run on steel rails. Train wheels have rims on the inside, and these guide the train along the rails. In this way trains really steer themselves.

■ The train follows the rails

▲ Rims on the wheels keep trains on the tracks.

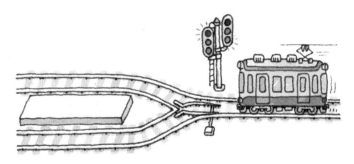

▲ When a track divides into two tracks, a switch will guide the train onto the right one.

● To the Parent

Operating an electric train differs from driving a car in that basically the only thing to control is speed. The brakes on an electric train are operated by hand. With his left hand the engineer manipulates the handle that increases and decreases speed, while his right hand controls the brake. Recently, however, more and more trains have only a single control for both power and brake. Small children might possibly think that these handles are for controlling direction. To help your child understand this concept correctly, you can compare the steering mechanism to a water faucet. You turn a knob to make the water flow faster or slower.

■ Levers in front of the driver control the train's speed; one is for "stop," and the other is for "go."

The lever on the left is for the power.
The driver turns it to start or to go faster.

To slow down or stop, the driver pulls
the brake lever on the right towards him.

Some types of drivers' seats

Wow! Look
at all the
levers and
switches.

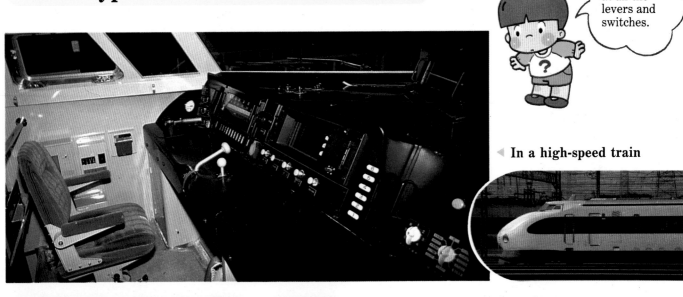

◀ **In a high-speed train**

▲ **The driver's seat in an
ordinary express train**

▲ **Controls a driver uses
in a new commuter train**

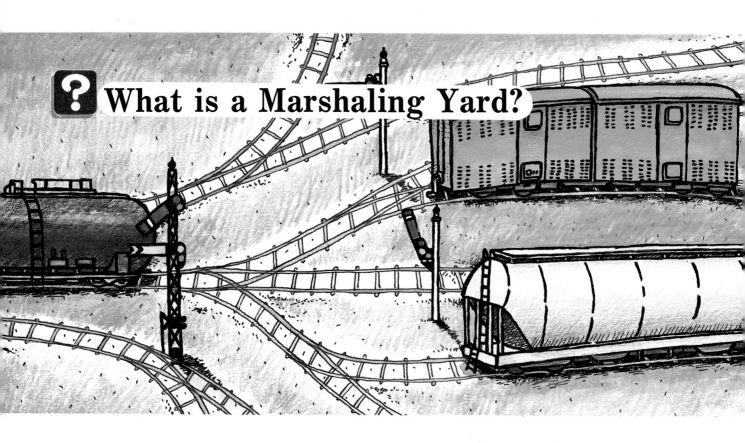

What is a Marshaling Yard?

(ANSWER) It is a huge place where boxcars are taken off of one freight train and put onto another train going in a different direction. Most freight starts in the city where it was manufactured or near the place where it was grown. But not all of it is going to the same place, so the railroads have these marshaling yards where the freight can be switched to trains going to where the freight is being sent. Some of this changing of cars is done in smaller switching yards, but on long-distance trains it is usually done in these marshaling yards.

▶ Many of the world's freight trains travel great distances through all sorts of terrain. This train, pulled by two locomotives, is passing through mountains in Canada. It carries different kinds of freight.

And what is a roundhouse?

When something goes wrong with a train it must be repaired. This is usually done in a roundhouse. The car is driven onto the rail in the center of the circle, and the turntable is turned so that the car can be put on any rail of the roundhouse to be repaired. Then it is driven out and put on a train.

● **To the Parent**

Railway freight trains in some countries may have as many as 150-200 boxcars loaded with many dozens of commodities destined for various locations. A train headed west from Chicago, for example, might be composed of 100 boxcars. These will go on a single train to a marshaling yard that is located outside of Chicago. There some boxcars will be removed from the train and put on other trains going in another direction. The marshaling yard has many tracks for switching cars from one train to another so that they eventually reach their destination. This cannot be done on ordinary tracks because it would interfere with operations of trains. These marshaling yards give railroads flexibility without which they would not be able to maintain their role as one of the cheapest methods of carrying goods overland.

How Does a Monorail Train Run With No Tracks?

▲ A monorail train glides along its single rail in a large city.

(ANSWER) The "mono" in monorail means one. So a monorail is a train that runs on one rail instead of two. It has rubber wheels, which help it run smoothly on the single rail. Monorails are not as noisy as regular trains.

The wheels on some monorails grip the sides of the rail. This type of monorail gives a smooth ride.

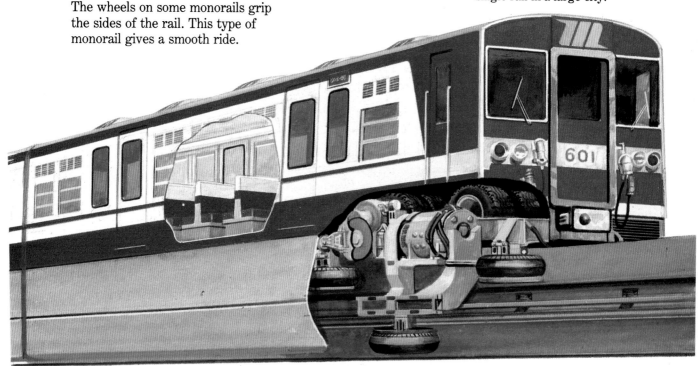

It rides on only one rail, just like me.

Load wheels

Guide wheels

Rail

This is a monorail where the cars hang down below the rail. It is called a hanging monorail. Hanging monorails have a simpler design than those that ride on top of the rail and are easier to build. But they sway a lot when you ride them.

They hang from a steel rail just like me. Am I a hanging monorail?

▲ This is a hanging monorail. It carries people over traffic that moves on the ground. Where are its wheels?

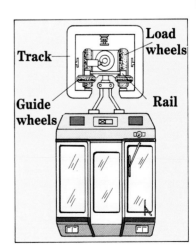

Track

Load wheels

Guide wheels

Rail

Why Are Seats in Cable Cars Built Just Like a Stairway?

ANSWER Cable cars go up and down a track on very steep hills. If the seats were on the same level, the passengers could fall off. Because the seats are built like steps, everyone is safe.

When the seats are built like steps, people can go up steep places safely.

This is what could happen if cable car seats were built on the same level.

■ What is a cable car like inside?

Here you can see how the passengers sit and how cable cars look underneath. Would you like to ride on one?

Oh, now I see how it works.

How Can a Cable Car Climb Up and Down Very Steep Places Without an Engine?

Cable cars do not have engines. They run on cables instead. They are joined to cables that wind around large wheels called pulleys. These cables pull the cars up and lower them down very steep hills.

This cable car is being pulled up the hill by the cable under it.

■ Cable cars of the world

◀ A cable car in Japan is coming out of a long tunnel.

This Swiss cable car has windows that look like stairs. ▶

• **To the Parent**

Cable cars are vehicles used for climbing up steep hills and mountains. They are extremely popular because of their distinctive box-like shape and for the verbal exchanges between riders when the up-bound and down-bound cars pass each other. Some mountain railways use a system in which a toothed rail that is set between the two track rails is engaged by a gear wheel mounted on the engine. This system is seen on mountain lines in Switzerland and was once used in Japan. The fact that cable cars are raised and lowered on thick cables does not yet seem to be generally known. This may be because track systems have overhead cables and pantographs, but these are used for electric lighting and telephones. At exactly the midway point between the top and bottom stations, the track forks to allow the cars to pass. In the unlikely event that the cable might break, the brakes of the cable car would be engaged automatically.

Have You Ever Seen a Steam Engine Puffing Smoke?

(ANSWER) For many years the steam engine was the king of the railroads. It puffed out clouds of smoke and made a loud chug-chugging sound as it moved along. The steam engine got its great power by burning coal. This turned water into steam, which was used to turn the wheels. Today there are very few steam engines left in the world that are working. But many can be seen in museums.

■ Some things you may not know about steam engines

When riding behind a steam engine in tunnels, passengers should never stick their heads out of the windows. It is very dangerous.

When a steam engine climbs steep hills, sand is poured onto the tracks to make them rough so that the wheels will not slip on the rails.

■ Steam engines from around the world

▶ Because this Swiss train must climb steep hills, engines on the line are used to push the trains from behind.

▼ On this railway line in Japan two steam engines are attached on the front of the trains to give them more power and speed.

Why Do We Need Train Tickets?

(ANSWER) People get on and off trains in different places. On many trains you pay for how far you want to go. Your ticket will tell the conductor where you got on and how far you are going.

▼ **An express-train ticket window in Southeast Asia**

▼ In many places you get a discount when you buy a special card valid for a set period or multiple rides.

■ Ticket machines

Some ticket machines automatically punch your ticket when you get on. You put the ticket in one end of the machine. It comes out the other with a small hole in it.

This subway in France uses ticket machines. The turnstile opens when you put your ticket into it. The rotating bars lock in place again when your ticket comes out the other end.

■ Ticket checking

Sometimes the conductor will pass through the train to check your ticket, so you must not lose it.

Busy terminals have long rows of ticket machines so that even during rush hours they can handle all the passengers in a very short time. If they did not have a great number of these automatic ticket sellers, passengers would have to stand in line for a long time just to buy a ticket. This is the main station in Bangkok, Thailand.

45

❓ Why Do Railways Have Signals?

ANSWER 1 It would be very dangerous if there were no traffic signals on railways. One train could crash into another head-on.

ANSWER 2 Railway traffic signals are also needed because one train could crash into the back of the train in front.

ANSWER 3 When there are traffic signals, we needn't worry. They tell us to stop for danger, or to go slow, or when it's safe to go fast.

Oh no! The trains are going to crash!!!

What Do the Colors of the Signals Tell Us?

Green tells us that the track ahead is clear and that it is safe for the train to travel at normal speeds.

Red tells us to stop because the track ahead is not clear. The driver will stop even if the track looks clear to him.

Yellow tells us that the train in front has passed the next signal point and that we can move ahead at slower speeds.

❓ Why Does a Ship Float?

ANSWER Water has the power to keep things afloat. If this power is greater than the weight of the ship, the ship will float. But if the ship is too heavy or gets full of water, it will sink.

TRY THIS

An experiment in the bath

When it is light it floats.

When you place an empty basin in the bath, it floats. The water's power forces it to float.

Look! It filled up with water and sank!

When the basin becomes filled with water, it sinks. The basin has become too heavy.

Ships Are Built to Keep Their Balance in the Water

Ship bottoms are shaped so that when a ship leans over, it always becomes level again.

The decks of ships act like covers to keep water from getting inside and making the ship too heavy.

When it has no cargo a ship floats high in the water.

Even when it is fully loaded, a ship will not sink. This is because the load line is still above the water.

Load line

● **To the Parent**

How is it that ships made of steel, which is heavier than wood, can float? To a child, nothing could be more mysterious. To understand how, we must remember the old Archimedean principle that when a body is immersed in water it is held up by a force equal to the weight of the water it displaces. We call this force buoyancy. Even a metal object, if it is shaped like a wash basin, for example, will be buoyant and float. But if it fills up with water, it will quickly sink.

49

What Makes a Ship Move?

ANSWER A ship's engines turn the propeller, which has blades like a fan. As the blades turn they push the water back and the ship moves forward.

▲ A ship's propeller

■ Some special ships move without propellers

▲ **Hydrofoil.** A very fast ship that gets its power as water is forced out of a jet.

▲ **Swamp buggy.** A large fan that pushes air backward makes this boat very speedy.

What Makes a Ship Turn?

▲ **Command post.** The captain of the ship stays on the bridge. Controls here can make the rudder move and turn the ship.

▲ **A ship's rudder.** When it is turned, the ship changes its direction.

> Heave ho! Here we go!

> Tugboats are small, but they're very strong pushers.

Large ships cannot move easily and need lots of room to turn. Inside a harbor, small boats called tugboats help them change their direction by pushing them this way or that way.

Some large ships have water jets called side thrusters to help them change direction.

● **To the Parent**

People have sailed the seas in wind-powered sailing ships for ages. The steam engine was invented in the 18th century, and the steamship came into use in the 19th century. Today most of the large ships are powered by diesel or turbine engines, with the propulsive force supplied by a propeller. It operates on the same principle as an ordinary electric fan, with curved blades rotating on a shaft. The propeller pushes water to the rear. Ships have no brakes, but if the direction of the propeller is reversed, the ship will stop and then begin to move to the rear. Since the variable-pitch propeller was put in use, it is not necessary to go into reverse to stop the ship. The rudder is used to change the direction that the ship is traveling and has not changed very much since the days of the sailing ships.

❓ How Do Sailboats Move?

A sailboat and a motorboat are sailing along together.

Oh dear, the wind has stopped and I can't move.

Bye-bye! I'll go on ahead.

ANSWER Sailboats move by catching the wind in their sails. Big ships that are powered by sails are called sailing ships. For thousands of years people used sailing ships to move cargo and to carry them on journeys all over the world. Later, engines were invented, and they were used to power ships.

▲ **Yachts.** These colorful sailboats are used for fun and racing.

Oh oh! My motor is dead.

Bye-bye! The wind is blowing again!

■ Large sailing ships use many sails to catch the wind

■ Sailing against the wind by following a zigzag course

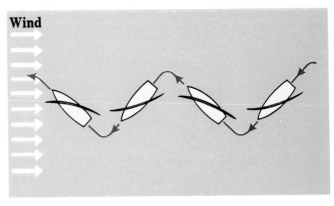

Wind

▲ By changing the direction of their sails, sailboats can sail into the wind as shown here. This is called tacking.

● To the Parent

Sailboats use the wind's power, but they do not just go the way the wind blows. The principle of sailing is much the same as that for airplane wings. The difference in pressure that develops when the wind passes the side of the sail that is filled with air and the opposite side results in a force akin to lift. The boat moves according to the sum of the forces that tend to make the hull move in a straight line and at an angle to the sails. Sailboats move easily with the wind but must run zigzag to move against it. They normally sail at roughly five knots but can sail at 10 knots or more provided that the wind is right. To take advantage of the wind, their sails are large compared to the hull. This makes them unstable so that a center-board is needed on the keel.

◀ A sailing ship cruising at sea.

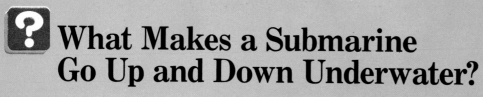

What Makes a Submarine Go Up and Down Underwater?

ANSWER Submarines have tanks inside. These are filled with water to make the submarine sink. To make the sub rise, they are emptied to make it lighter.

When a submarine is underwater its tanks are filled. It can go down very deep to where it is inky dark.

543

543

Water tank

● **To the Parent**

Submarines have been used since the 18th Century, but the first practical submarine was not built until just prior to World War I. Today most submarines are in military service, but future plans call for the use of submarine oil tankers. Submarines submerge and surface by filling or emptying their seawater tanks, but they also control their depth with a horizontal rudder. The tanks shown here have been simplified. The actual tanks are at the hull's periphery.

54

I've emptied my tanks and am back on the surface. But I can stay underwater for more than a day if I want to.

Let's have a look at what's inside this submarine down below us.

Control room
Where orders are given to the people who work in the submarine, and where the submarine is steered.

Dining
Here's where the crew members eat their meals.

Crew's cabin
Where the crew sleep and relax.

Did You Know That Some Ships Can Come Up on Land?

ANSWER A Hovercraft travels on the sea but can also move over flat land. It rides on a cushion of air that is blown down against the surface beneath it, which can be water or land. The Hovercraft is driven forward by one or more propellers like those shown here.

▲ **A giant Hovercraft crossing the English Channel**

It rides on a cushion of air blown downward.

Look! When it stops to rest, the air bag goes flat.

No air is blown downward when it stops, so the air bag collapses.

56

Planes and Cars That Can Run on the Water

Amphibious rescue craft

This plane can land on either the sea or the land, which is why it is called amphibious. It is used to rescue people who have had accidents at sea. It has pontoons on its wings for moving on water.

Look at that! A plane that can land anywhere!

Amphibious car. It travels on roads like other cars, but it also drives in the water like a boat.

● **To the Parent**

Perhaps the best-known amphibious vehicle is the Hovercraft, which forces air downward beneath its hull at high pressure and creates an air cushion. It is driven forward by propellers. It is somewhat like a cross between a ship and an airplane and can run not only over water but over any reasonably flat land area. A prototype of the vessel was built and operated by the Finnish engineer Toivo J. Kaario in 1935. It was in the mid-1950s that Sir Christopher Cockerell, a British electronics engineer, first applied the name Hovercraft to this means of transportation. It first went into regular service on the Strait of Dover, making the trip in a scant 50 minutes, a crossing that had required two hours when it had to be made by ferry.

❓ Are There Traffic Rules for Ships?

ANSWER Ships travel on the sea in shipping lanes. When
traveling in these lanes, especially in narrow straits
and near ports and harbors, there are traffic rules
to make sure that ships do not bump into one another.
These rules are the same everywhere in the world.

■ Traffic rules for ships at sea

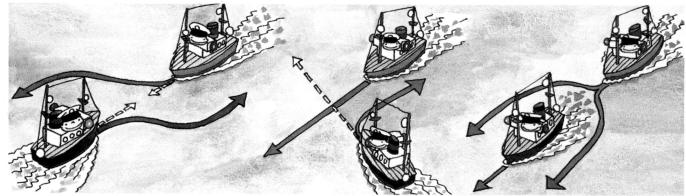

▲ When two ships are coming
towards each other, both
must move to the right.

▲ When a ship is crossing the
path of another, the other
turns and goes behind it.

▲ One ship may pass another
on either side if it
signals with its whistle.

How Do Ships Travel at Night?

Ships traveling at night use lighthouses as guideposts. They also use radar to improve safety. Ships have a red light on the left (or port) side and a green light on the right (or starboard) side. All these things help ships travel safely when it is dark or there is fog.

● **To the Parent**

Despite the vastness of the oceans, merchant shipping generally has to follow routes that are predetermined. In straits and harbors and the approaches to them, where ship traffic is heavy, passage is restricted. Strict rules are implemented to prevent ships from colliding. These rules apply everywhere that ships travel. One of these is that on the water, traffic keeps to the right. Ships keep track of their positions with charts and by observing various traditional markers such as mountains, lighthouses, the sun and stars. Today positions can be accurately maintained with the help of man-made satellites. Thus ships are able to make safe voyages day and night under all sorts of weather conditions.

? How Does an Airplane Fly?

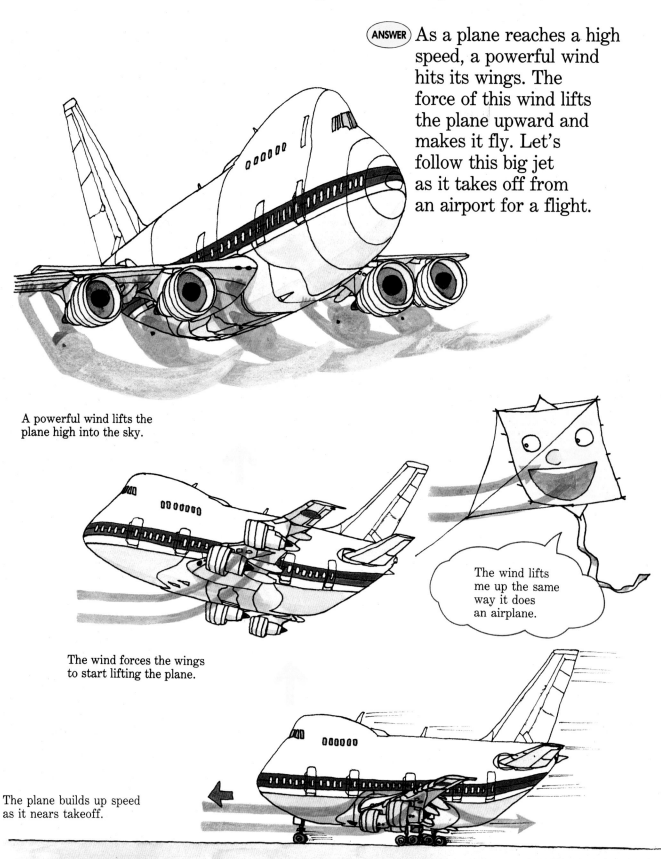

ANSWER As a plane reaches a high speed, a powerful wind hits its wings. The force of this wind lifts the plane upward and makes it fly. Let's follow this big jet as it takes off from an airport for a flight.

A powerful wind lifts the plane high into the sky.

The wind lifts me up the same way it does an airplane.

The wind forces the wings to start lifting the plane.

The plane builds up speed as it nears takeoff.

How Airplane Parts Work

The action of the wind on different parts of the plane makes it turn, climb or come down.

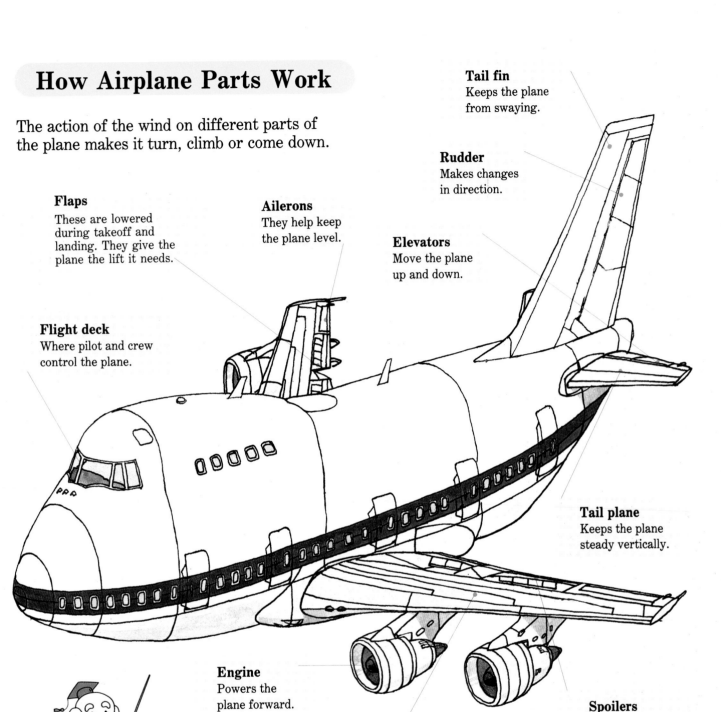

Tail fin
Keeps the plane from swaying.

Rudder
Makes changes in direction.

Flaps
These are lowered during takeoff and landing. They give the plane the lift it needs.

Ailerons
They help keep the plane level.

Elevators
Move the plane up and down.

Flight deck
Where pilot and crew control the plane.

Tail plane
Keeps the plane steady vertically.

Engine
Powers the plane forward.

Main wing
Lifts the plane into the air.

Spoilers
Act like brakes to slow the plane down.

• **To the Parent**

When an airplane flies, the air hitting the wing is divided into streams passing above and below. Since wings are normally curved on the upper surface and flat on the lower, the upper stream of air has farther to travel and moves faster. Thus the air pressure exerted on the upper surface is less than that on the lower. This difference is called lift, and the amount of it that is produced by a wing is proportional to the square of the speed. The faster a plane flies, the greater the lift. When the speed drops the lift is also reduced. To maintain sufficient lift during takeoff and landing, the nose of the plane is kept somewhat higher.

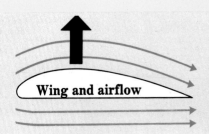

Wing and airflow

❓ How Does a Helicopter Fly?

(ANSWER) A helicopter flies by the turning of its rotor. The rotor blades are like wings. When they turn fast, they give the power needed for takeoff.

■ Helicopter rotors can have different numbers of blades

▲ A helicopter with a 2-blade rotor.

▲ A medium-size helicopter with a 3-blade rotor.

▲ This helicopter with a 4-blade rotor can carry many people.

They Fly in Any Direction

By tilting the rotor to the left or right, the
pilot can move the helicopter in either direction.

Tilting the rotor to the front or rear makes
the helicopter fly forwards or backwards.

Look at this!
A helicopter
powered by
a rubber band.
Isn't it neat?

Helicopters can stop even in midair.
That makes them very useful to us.

To the Parent

A helicopter obtains lift from the large propeller on
top called a rotor. It does not need forward speed
to obtain lift the way an airplane does, but can rise
straight up and hover in midair. When the rotor is
tilted the helicopter will change direction. Just as
when you fly a whirligig on an angle, there are two
forces: vertical, or lift; and horizontal, or propulsive
force. A smaller, horizontally oriented propeller on
the tail acts to prevent the body of the helicopter
from spinning in the opposite direction to the main
rotor and aids the helicopter in changing direction.

Just How Big Is a Boeing 747?

ANSWER A 747 jumbo jet is wide enough to allow 10 passengers to sit in a row across the plane. Altogether some 500 people can be carried on short flights. When fully loaded a 747 weighs about 385 tons (350 t).

❶ The body of a 747 jumbo jet is about 230 feet (70 m) long. As you can see here, the plane is as long as three cars on a train.

❷ From wing tip to wing tip a 747 measures nearly 200 feet (60 m). A two-engine plane could fit on the wing of one of these jumbo jets.

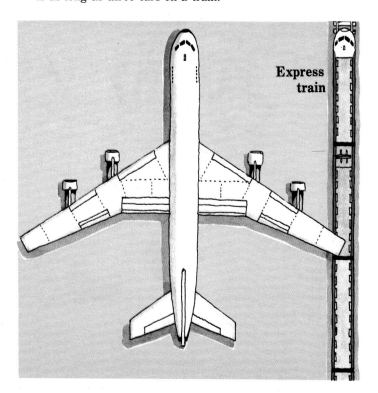

Express train

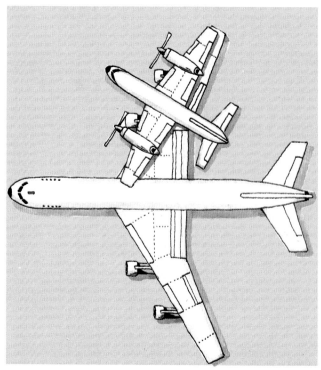

❸ From the ground to the tip of the tail fin the 747 measures almost 65 feet (20 m). That is about as tall as a building with five floors.

❹ A 747 has 18 wheels, and each is 4 feet (1.25 m) high. Each of the 747's engine fans is 8 feet (2.5 m) across. A man looks tiny on one of them.

● **To the Parent**

The Boeing 747 is the world's largest passenger plane. It weighs about 193 tons (175 t). When fully fueled and loaded with passengers and baggage, its weight doubles. The 747 was built to handle greater numbers of airline passengers without sacrificing speed. The exact number of passengers per plane depends on the length of the flight. On very long trips the number of passengers is reduced so the plane can take on extra fuel. For this reason long-distance international travel planes are usually shorter and are equipped with 350 to 400 seats. For the shorter domestic routes they frequently have as many as 500 seats. Because this is more than double the capacity of a typical four-engine passenger jet, the 747 has made travel by airline more economical.

❓ What Are Cargo Planes?

ANSWER Cargo planes are built for easy loading and unloading of freight. They have larger doors than passenger planes, and the deck is lower in the body. Sometimes the tail swings aside or down or the nose opens for easier loading.

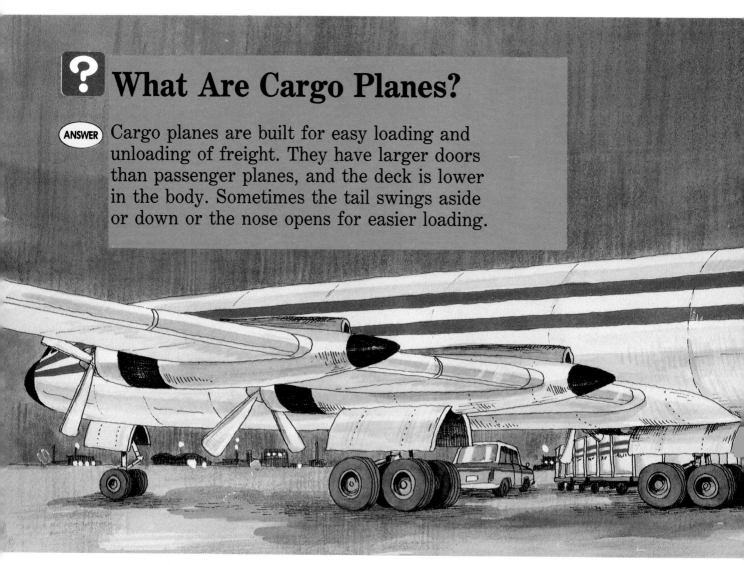

Some cargo planes

▲ **The Super Guppy**

This plane, which is flown by the National Aeronautics and Space Administration, is able to carry rocket engines and large airplane bodies. When fully loaded it weighs about 85 tons (77 t).

▲ The Super Guppy gets its name because it looks a little like a fish that is called a guppy.

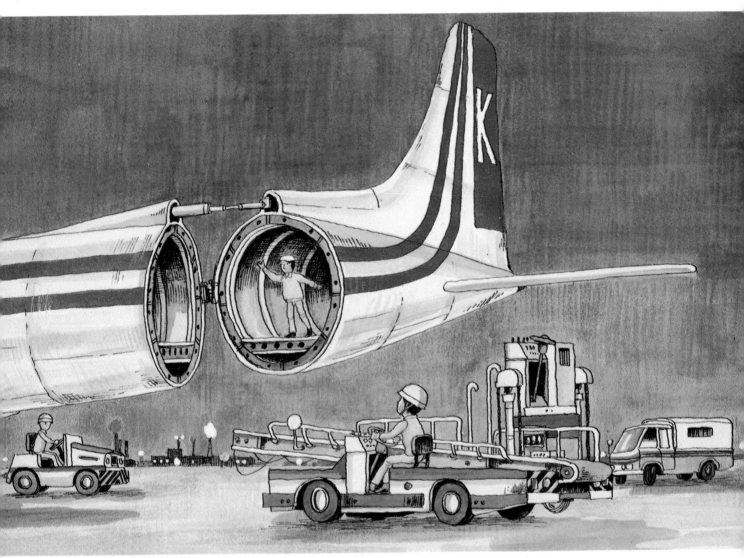

▲ This 747 jet is for carrying cargo only. The nose of the plane opens as if it were a mouth.

● To the Parent

Cargo planes have lower floors, which allow them to carry very large or heavy items of freight and make them easier to load and unload. Almost all military transport planes open at the rear of the fuselage so that trucks or loaders can be driven on and off. Cargo planes that have been modified from passenger versions have doors on the sides. Sometimes the nose and tail sections of these airplanes open on hinges.

? How Do Planes Take Off From Ships?

ANSWER To take off from an aircraft carrier, a plane has to get up enough speed. Since the decks are rather short, the planes must use a catapult, which gives them the extra boost they need to take off.

A plane ready for take-off. You can see the catapult.

How in the World Do the Planes Land?

A hook on the back of the plane catches on a cable and helps the plane stop.

▲ A plane ready to land on an aircraft carrier. Can you see its hook?

▲ Here it's just about to touch down.

• To the Parent

An airplane has to get up speed on a runway until it has enough lift to take off. Since the flight deck on even the largest carriers is fairly short, most planes could not take off without some help from steam-driven catapults, which accelerate them to take-off speed. Large aircraft carriers have four of these catapults and can launch planes rapidly one after another. Since planes normally cannot come to a quick stop, a steel cable is stretched across the deck during landing operations. It engages a hook that protrudes from the bottom rear of the aircraft carrier and thus halts the plane. Big carriers can carry as many as 90 planes. They roam the seas at will, and this makes them an important military force.

▲ The hook catches on the cable. This stops the plane in a short distance.

■ Where are the planes kept?

◄▲ Under the carrier's deck is a large area called a hangar. The planes are moved between the deck and hangar by very large elevators.

❓ How Does a Hot-Air Balloon Fly?

ANSWER When air becomes warm, it becomes lighter. In
a hot-air balloon, the air inside the balloon is
heated by burning gas. This hot air is lighter than
the air outside and causes the balloon to rise.

▲ A hot-air balloon getting
ready by burning gas.

● **To the Parent**

When air is heated it expands, and its specific gravity decreases. In a hot-air balloon a gas burner is mounted inside to heat the air, which provides lift. To descend, the burner is turned off and the air gradually cools. Direction can be changed only by selecting a different air current. The principle of balloon flight had been known long before two French brothers named Montgolfier built a hot-air balloon and flew it on Nov. 21, 1783. They were the first humans to fly through the air. In the 19th century, people began sealing hydrogen, a gas that is lighter than air, inside balloons and lifting them with engines. These dirigibles were popular in the 1930s but soon lost out to faster, safer travel by airplane.

How Do Balloons Go From Here to There?

A hot-air balloon goes where the wind blows, so it must catch a flow of air that is blowing in the direction it wants to go. To do that, it moves higher or lower.

71

How Does the Space Shuttle Get Into Space?

ANSWER On earth, engines use the oxygen in the air to burn fuel. But there is no oxygen in space, so rockets need to carry their own oxygen supply. The space shuttle goes into space with the help of powerful booster rockets, a giant fuel tank and its own supply of oxygen so its engines will operate in space.

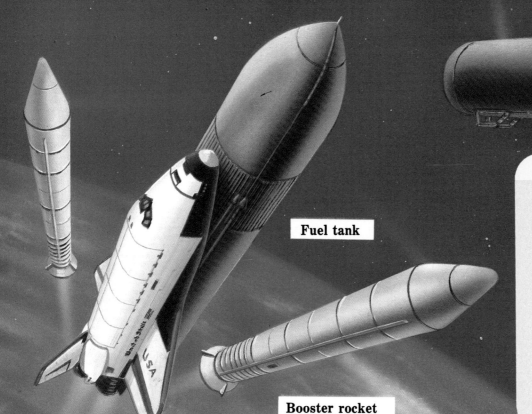

Fuel tank

Booster rocket

Why Can't Planes Also Go Into Space?

I wish I could go there too.

Airplane engines need air. But there is no air in space, so they can't go there.

When Will We Travel in Space?

ANSWER No exact time is known right now, but many people think it will soon be possible for us to travel in space. Then we'll travel by ships and buses in space just as we do on earth.

Space bus

Earth shuttle flights

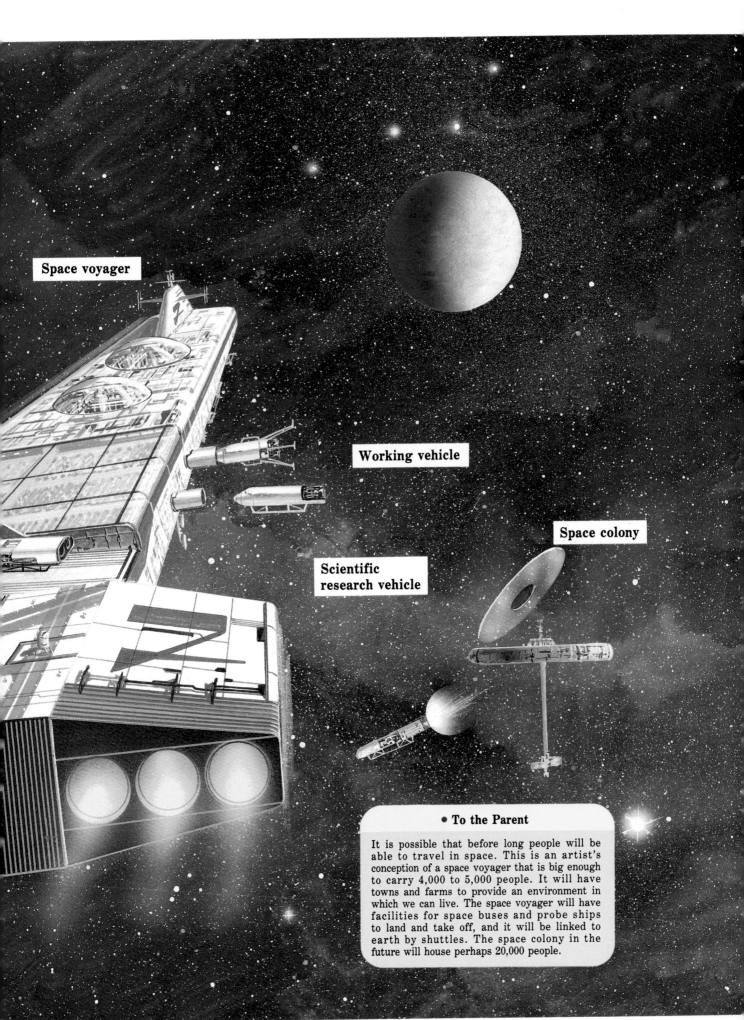

Space voyager

Working vehicle

Space colony

Scientific
research vehicle

● **To the Parent**

It is possible that before long people will be
able to travel in space. This is an artist's
conception of a space voyager that is big enough
to carry 4,000 to 5,000 people. It will have
towns and farms to provide an environment in
which we can live. The space voyager will have
facilities for space buses and probe ships
to land and take off, and it will be linked to
earth by shuttles. The space colony in the
future will house perhaps 20,000 people.

What Are Some Odd Ways That Vehicles Carry Other Vehicles?

(ANSWER) Vehicles are used mainly to carry people or cargo. But sometimes vehicles are used to carry other vehicles, as these pictures show.

▲ **Space shuttle and 747 jet**
The space shuttle gets a piggyback ride on the big jet. After it returns from space and lands in California, this is how the shuttle is taken to Florida, from where it will be sent into space again.

▲ **Locomotive and passenger train**
The passenger train here is not running by itself. It is being taken from the factory by a separate locomotive.

▲ **Helicopter and truck**
Helicopters can carry loads where they are needed, even where there are no roads.

● **To the Parent**

This is an unusual collection of photos showing vehicles being carried by other vehicles. The photo of the space shuttle and its 747 carrier was taken during a shuttle glide test. The hot-air balloon is used to lift the hang glider high into the air when there is no wind at lower altitudes. Each of the scenes, representing particular cases carried out in limited places, provides an interesting study in contrasts. For example, who would ever think that a truck driver would "drive" a train?

▲ Truck-trailer and express train coach

This coach for a super express train has wheels that are too far apart for it to travel on ordinary train rails. So it must be taken to where it is going by special trucks like this and by big ships.

▲ Truck-trailer and yacht

Here we see a pretty red and white yacht being hauled to the sea by a large truck with a special trailer. The mast, which holds the sails, is on top of the yacht.

▲ Hot-air balloon and hang glider

A hang glider can be flown only from high and windy places. This one is being taken up to where it is able to fly. It is carried high into the sky by a hot-air balloon.

▲ Car and glider

A glider has no power of its own. It must be pulled by something until it is going fast enough that it can fly alone. This car is going to pull the glider with a rope.

❓ What's This?

■ A ship to clean up oil spills

Isn't this a funny looking ship? Can you tell which way it is going? This is a ship for cleaning up oil that has been spilled on the sea. Both parts of the ship move forward together to trap oil between them. It is like an ordinary ship in the photo on the right.

■ Fold-away motorcycle

This motorcycle is handy. The seat and handlebars fold away so you can easily carry it in the trunk of a car. When you want to ride, you unfold them as shown here.

◼ Spines for safety

This railway car has many spines sticking out on top and down the sides. It is used by railways when they lay track or build bridges and tunnels. The spines are used to make measurements to ensure that there is enough room for trains to pass safely.

◼ Commuter car

This little car carries only one person. It doesn't use much gas or need much room to park. As our roads get more crowded, cars like this will be needed.

![?] And What Are These?

■ A pedal plane

This is an airplane that is powered by a person. It has pedals like a bicycle. When you pedal, the propeller turns. The plane is very light, and its propeller blades are large.

■ Energy-saving race

This is a race in which people try to go as far as they can using as little fuel as possible. The cars are lightweight and have wheels like those on bicycles. They can carry only one person.

Growing-Up Album

Which Ones Have You Ridden On?

Here are a variety of vehicles your child may
have ridden on. Mark as appropriate, and
record the date, child's age and your comments.

Baby carriage

Tricycle

Bicycle

Car

Taxi

Bus

Express train

Ordinary train

■ Notes about the rides

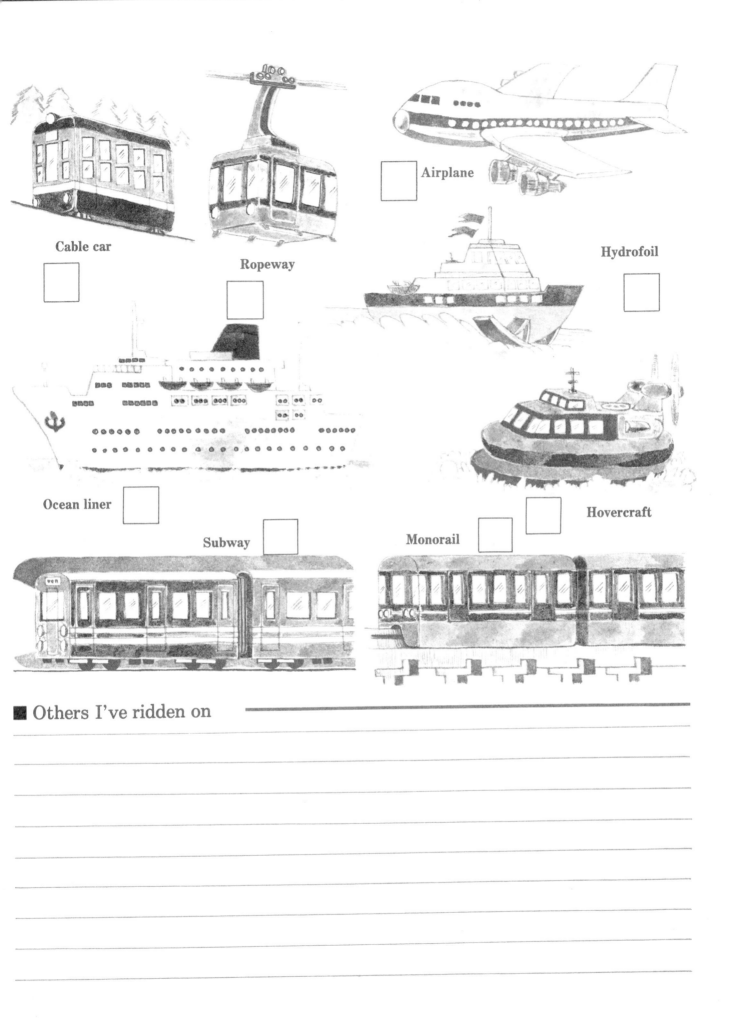

Airplane ☐

Cable car

Ropeway

Hydrofoil ☐

Ocean liner ☐

Subway ☐

Monorail ☐

Hovercraft

■ Others I've ridden on

Travel Album

When did your child take his or her first long
trip, and on what types of vehicles? What
were the child's reactions? You can make a
meaningful souvenir of the trip by pasting
into this album one or more pictures that
were taken, along with tickets that may
have been used for buses or trains, or
even for rides or shows at amusement parks.

Paste a photograph here

Paste a photograph here

What Kind of Vehicle Am I?

All sorts of vehicles like to boast about what they do. But which vehicle is speaking? Put on your thinking cap and see if you can find the right vehicle among the pictures here. Point to it and say its right name. Have your child find the right vehicle. Each of the vehicles on these pages explains something about what it does in numbers 1 to 8. Have the child guess which vehicle goes with which number.

1. I make a loud noise with my siren and bell so other cars get out of the way.

2. I make an ee-o, ee-o sound and flash my red light as I move.

3. I'm very strong and push earth or stone around.

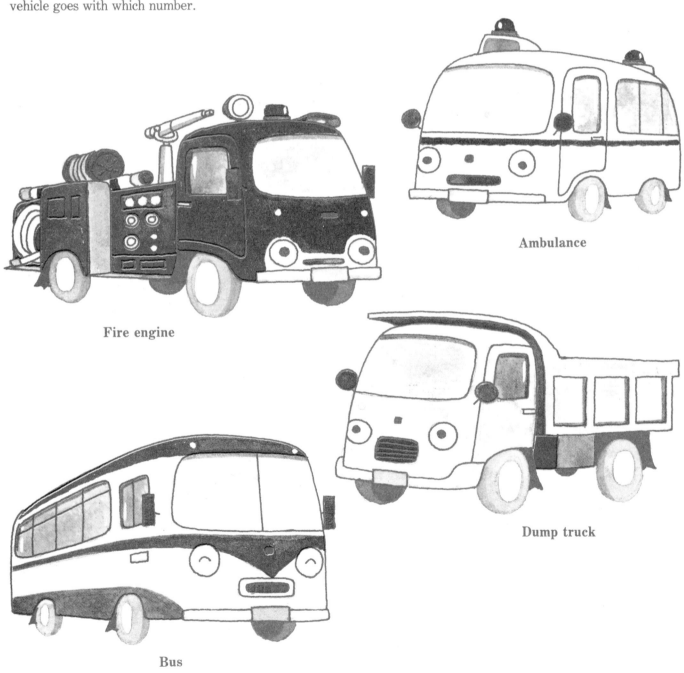

Fire engine

Ambulance

Dump truck

Bus

4. I can **carry** lots of people at one time.

5. I have **a** box on my back that I can lift up to empty out a **load** of earth or stones.

6. I have **a** drum on me that turns round and round.

7. I can **lift** things up and put them in high places.

8. I carry letters and packages.

How many did your child guess correctly? Here are the answers:
1. Fire engine
2. Ambulance
3. Bulldozer
4. Bus
5. Dump truck
6. Ready-mix concrete truck
7. Mobile crane
8. Mail truck

Mobile crane

Mail truck

Ready-mix concrete truck

Bulldozer

A Child's First Library of Learning

Wheels and Wings

TIME
LIFE ®

Time-Life Books Inc. is a wholly owned subsidiary of
Time Incorporated.
Time-Life Books, Alexandria, Virginia
Children's Publishing

Director:	Robert H. Smith
Associate Director:	R. S. Wotkyns III
Editorial Director:	Neil Kagan
Promotion Director:	Kathleen Tresnak
Editorial Consultants:	Jacqueline A. Ball
	Andrew Gutelle

Editorial Supervision by:
International Editorial Services Inc.
Tokyo, Japan

Editor:	C. E. Berry
Editorial Research:	Miki Ishii
Design:	Kim Bolitho
Writer:	Pauline Bush
Educational Consultants:	Janette Bryden
	Laurie Hanawa
Translation:	Ronald K. Jones

Library of Congress Cataloging in Publication Data
Wheels and wings.
    p.   cm. — (A Child's first library of learning)
    Summary: Provides answers to questions about bikes, cars,
trucks, trains, ships, submarines, planes, and rockets, including
how they are built, why they work, and how to operate them
safely. An activities section is included.
    ISBN 0-8094-4861-0.   ISBN 0-8094-4862-9 (lib. bdg.)
    1. Vehicles—Miscellanea—Juvenile literature.
[1. Vehicles—Miscellanea.   2. Questions and answers.]
I. Time-Life Books.   II. Series.
TL147.W488 1988   629.04—dc19   88-20174
©1988 Time-Life Books Inc.
©1983 Gakken Co. Ltd.

Third printing 1990. Printed in U.S.A.
Published simultaneously in Canada.

TIME-LIFE is a trademark of Time Incorporated U.S.A.

Time-Life Books Inc. offers a wide range of fine publications,
including home video products. For subscription information, call
1-800-621-7026 or write TIME-LIFE BOOKS, P.O. Box C-32068,
Richmond, Virginia 23261-2068.